Easter

Story and pictures by **Miriam Nerlove**

ALBERT WHITMAN & COMPANY, MORTON GROVE, ILLINOIS

For my family with love,
and special thanks to Judith.

Text and illustrations © 1989 by Miriam Nerlove.
Published in 1989 by Albert Whitman & Company,
6340 Oakton Street, Morton Grove, Illinois 60053.
Published simultaneously in Canada by
General Publishing, Limited, Toronto.
Printed in the United States of America.
10 9 8 7 6 5 4 3 2

Library of Congress Cataloging-in-Publication Data

Nerlove, Miriam.
Easter/written and illustrated by Miriam Nerlove.
p.   cm.
Summary: Rhyming text follows two children as they celebrate
Easter with their family by decorating eggs, enjoying Easter
baskets, going to church, and returning home to an egg hunt and
Easter dinner.
ISBN 0-8075-1871-9 (hardcover)
ISBN 0-8075-1872-7 (paperback)
1. Easter—Juvenile literature. [1. Easter.] I. Title.
BV55.N457 1989   89-35394
263'.93—dc20   CIP
                                                          AC

When spring arrives and Easter's here,
it feels just like a brand new year!

Winter's gone, so is the snow.
The grass and flowers start to grow.

Shh! Let's be quiet—not a sound.
The Easter bunny's hopping round.

We boil some eggs on Saturday,
and color them in just this way:

we use our crayons and special dye.
What a mess we make. Oh, my!

By Easter Sunday's morning light,
we find what Bunny left last night:

some baskets filled with jelly beans,
and chocolate eggs with yellow cream.

Now let's put on your Easter dress,
so you can look your very best.

Add bright black shoes and lacy socks,
and take your new hat from the box.

Gram and Gramps have come today.
We're off to church to sing and pray.

Inside the church the lilies bloom.
Can you smell their sweet perfume?
We hear the Easter story soon...

We think of the Friday Jesus died,
when people felt so sad inside.

Women came to his tomb at dawn
on Easter Sunday—he was gone!

The tombstone had been rolled away.
An angel came to them to say,

"Jesus Christ has risen today!"

Back at home we watch and wait…
Our family's here. Let's celebrate!

The Easter dinner tastes so good,
we eat more than we thought we could!

Then Daddy disappears outside—
we think he took some eggs to hide.

Let's hunt for eggs—look over there.

Easter eggs are everywhere!

But still, there's one thing left to do—

Let's share a candy egg or two!